DOMESTIC VIOLENCE

Joe Layden

THE MILLBROOK PRESS
Brookfield, Connecticut

Published by The Millbrook Press, Inc.
2 Old New Milford Road
Brookfield, CT 06804
© 1994 Blackbirch Graphics, Inc.

5 4 3 2 1

Created and produced in association with Blackbirch Graphics.
Series Editor: Tanya Lee Stone

Library of Congress Cataloging-in-Publication Data
Layden, Joe.
    Domestic violence / Joe Layden.
        p.   cm. — (Headliners)
    Includes bibliographical references and index.
    Summary: Discusses domestic violence, including chapters on victims, batterers, and breaking free from the abuse.
        ISBN 1-56294-554-8
        1. Family violence—United States—Juvenile literature.
    [1. Family violence.]   I. Title.   II. Series.
    HQ809.3.U5L39   1995
    362.82'92—dc20   94-36123
                                                                                            CIP
                                                                                            AC

Contents

Chapter 7

Exposing the Horror

Early in the morning on Wednesday, July 6, 1994, twenty-one-year-old Janice Dickson of Syracuse, New York, found herself in the middle of a heated argument with her boyfriend, forty-one-year-old Jimmie Lee McRae. This was not unusual for them. Dickson and McRae had a stormy relationship, and over the previous two years they had often argued bitterly. Occasionally, the disagreements had blown up into physical fights. The police had been called to Dickson and McRae's home as far back as 1991, to investigate incidents of domestic violence, but Dickson always was unwilling to press charges against McRae.

Friends and family had urged Dickson to leave McRae before she was seriously hurt, but she refused. She said that she loved him, and she hoped one day that they would be married and have a family together.

That never happened. The final fight between Dickson and McRae ended terribly. McRae told police in a signed statement that while he shook Dickson by the shoulders, her head hit a wall, knocking her unconscious. As she lay on the floor, he hit her across the chest with a stick. When paramedics arrived on the scene, they discovered Dickson on her back, surrounded by glass from a broken beer bottle. She was pronounced dead at 12:32 A.M.

Each year, millions of Americans are victims of domestic violence.

Opposite:
In 1994, the O. J. Simpson murder case brought the issue of domestic violence into the spotlight. Here, the press watches as Simpson arrives at a Los Angeles courthouse in a police van.

Later that same day, McRae pleaded not guilty to charges of murder and criminal possession of a weapon. "She chose to remain in this relationship," Captain Richard Walsh of the Syracuse City Police Department told the Syracuse *Post-Standard*. "Unfortunately, it ended the way many of these relationships do."

Sadly, the story of Janice Dickson is not unique. Each year in the United States, millions of women, children, and men are emotionally and physically abused by the

Demonstrators call attention to the problem of family violence at a 1992 rally in Marin County, California. Protests such as these are often organized to urge lawmakers to pass stricter laws regarding domestic violence.

people they care most about—their husbands or wives, parents, children, boyfriends or girlfriends. Many of these incidents, however, go unreported—for a variety of reasons. The complexities of family relationships, the social stigma that is attached to domestic and family violence, and a criminal justice system that fails to adequately protect the victim contribute to this problem. As Health and Human Services Secretary Donna Shalala noted in a 1994 episode of the show *Face the Nation*, "Domestic violence is an unacknowledged epidemic in our society."

It is a problem that has a long history of going largely unnoticed; worse, domestic violence has been either ignored or tolerated. Only once in a great while does an incident arise that casts a national spotlight upon the issue of domestic violence. The 1994 O. J. Simpson case was one such incident.

The O. J. Simpson Case

On the night of Friday, June 17, 1994, millions of people sat transfixed watching a larger-than-life human drama unfolding on television before their eyes. There was forty-seven-year-old O. J. Simpson—football star, movie actor, broadcaster, millionaire—running from the law, cruising down a Los Angeles freeway in his friend's white Ford Bronco, holding a gun to his own head.

It seemed at the time to be the final act of desperation by a man whose life had fallen apart. Very early on the morning of Monday, June 13, the bodies of thirty-five-year-old Nicole Brown Simpson, Simpson's ex-wife, and twenty-five-year-old Ronald Goldman, a friend of Nicole's, were discovered outside Nicole's townhouse in Brentwood, California.

Simpson quickly became the primary suspect in the case, and, by Friday morning, police were prepared to arrest him. But instead of surrendering to authorities as planned, Simpson fled his Brentwood mansion with Al Cowlings, a

The police pursuit of O. J. Simpson, a passenger in the white Ford Bronco (bottom left), was shown live on network television.

friend and former National Football League teammate. That afternoon, Simpson's friend, Robert Kardashian, read a note from O. J. In the note, Simpson not only proclaimed his innocence, but also described himself as a "battered husband." This was a reference to publicity surrounding the murder and his relationship with Nicole. Two days before the arrest, Los Angeles police had released reports of previous incidents during which O. J. had been accused of abusing Nicole Brown Simpson. To the general public, accustomed to seeing Simpson only as a smiling, happy, successful man, the report was stunning.

The report revealed that on New Year's Day, 1989, when the Simpsons were still married, Simpson beat his wife so severely that she required hospital treatment. When authorities arrived at his house, he yelled at the men, "The police have been out here eight times before, and now you're going to arrest me for this? This is a family matter. Why do you want to make a big deal out of this?"

Simpson later pleaded no contest to misdemeanor spousal battery (the act of beating) charges, served no jail time, paid a small fine, and was even allowed to receive counseling over the phone by a psychiatrist of his choice. The case went virtually unnoticed. But after Nicole Brown Simpson's murder, the incident received new attention.

So, too, did tapes of a 911 call made by Nicole Brown Simpson in the fall of 1993. At the time, she and O. J. were divorced, but were still spending a lot of time together. O. J. and Nicole often attended public functions as a couple and were reportedly considering a reconciliation. On the night of the call to 911, though, Simpson was angry. He was heard on the 911 tape screaming at Nicole, shouting obscenities while she cried and asked for help. It was a chilling recording, one that led many people to believe that Simpson was indeed capable of killing his former wife.

The 911 tape from 1993 also sparked a renewed dedication in people to examine the issue of domestic violence. Suddenly, a popular, admired public figure was discovered to have a history of abusing his wife and was charged with the crime of murder. Domestic violence became a central issue in the Simpson case, and it led many people to feel that if a man like O. J. Simpson could be a batterer, anyone could.

Perhaps the one positive thing that came out of this terrible tragedy was that domestic violence was seen as a major problem in our society. The idea that this kind of violence knows no boundaries—economic or societal—needed to be talked about. And America did talk. Radio shows, magazines, network news programs, newspapers—all focused on the issue of domestic violence in the days and weeks following the deaths of Nicole Brown Simpson and Ronald Goldman. And, maybe more importantly, calls to domestic violence telephone "hotlines" (telephone numbers a person can call for help) increased dramatically. In Los Angeles, hotline calls were up 80 percent. All

O. J. Simpson in court. The publicity surrounding his trial drew national attention to the "unacknowledged epidemic" of domestic violence.

around the country, shelters for battered women reported record numbers of calls. Calls poured in, not only from people finally ready to acknowledge the horror of their own situation, but from people who wondered if they might be abusing their partners without even realizing it.

Although the circumstances that led to this reaction were tragic, now at least there was a new opportunity to change the way people viewed violence in the home; there was a chance to mobilize the forces against a disease known as domestic violence.

What Is Domestic Violence?

The term "domestic violence" is typically used to describe the abuse of one family member by another. Domestic violence occurs in all of the many types of families that exist. No matter what the living situation is—two married adults with or without children, unmarried couples, extended families sharing a home—domestic violence is a serious problem.

Victims typically suffer from one or more of three main forms of domestic violence:

Physical Abuse. This involves aggressive, harmful, physical contact, such as punching, kicking, biting, or choking. Assaults with weapons are common.

Sexual Abuse. Sexual abuse is a form of violence in which sex is used in a hurtful or unhealthy way, usually to degrade, intimidate, or otherwise harm the victim. Forced sexual activity is an act of aggression and power, and it is a form of domestic violence. When one spouse sexually abuses the other, it is also referred to as "marital rape." According to the American Humane Association, women are most often the victims of sexual abuse. One out of ten women, for example, is the victim of incest by the time she is eighteen.

Emotional/Psychological Abuse. While this type of abuse is not physical, it is highly destructive. It involves

Family violence is devastating for all involved. Often, no family member is spared in a violent household.

one person intentionally and systematically destroying the self-esteem of another, either through insults, intimidation, gestures, or control.

Statistics on domestic violence in America are staggering. The American Humane Association estimates that nearly 34 out of every 1,000 American children are abused in some way. And, the Department of Health and Human Services reports that more than 3 children die in the United States each day from abuse and neglect.

"Family violence is the root cause of virtually every major social problem we face as a nation today," Sarah Buel, a Boston prosecutor of domestic violence cases, said in response to a 1994 American Bar Association report on the effect of domestic violence on children. "It is in our homes that children learn that it's OK to use violence to get what you want."

According to the *Journal of the American Medical Association* (JAMA), domestic violence is the leading cause of injury and death among American women, more common than automobile accidents, muggings, and cancer deaths combined. Because so many cases go unreported, statistics vary, but the National Council on Child Abuse and Family Violence in Washington, D.C., estimates that each year between 3 and 4 million women in the United States are battered by their husbands and partners. That means that one incident occurs every 15 seconds, witnessed by as many as 10 million children. Of the 5,745 women murdered in 1991, roughly 60 percent were killed by someone they knew; half were murdered by a spouse or

Children are often victims of family violence. In the United States, 34 out of every 1,000 children suffer from abuse.

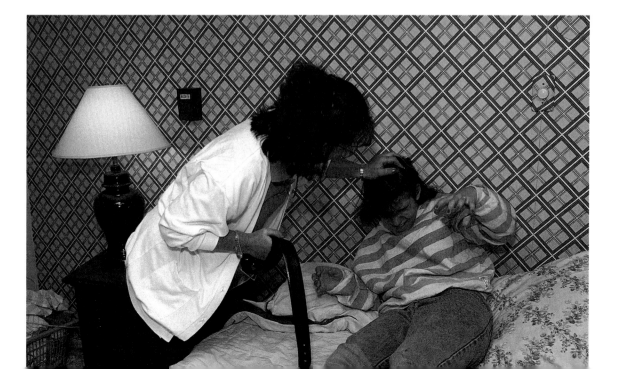

Signs of Abuse

There are many signs of abuse. In some states, teachers are requested to be on the lookout for these signs. Here are some things to look for: A person who has been subjected to long-term physical abuse will often have injuries and bruises caused by severe beatings. Being hit with a belt, stick, board, or other heavy object is one form of physical abuse. Other forms of physical abuse include being burned, held under water, tied up, severely shaken, or locked out of the house. Black eyes, welts, burn marks, and bleeding are common signs that physical abuse is taking place. In the case of abuse of elderly people, signs of neglect also include dirty clothes, body odor, matted hair, missing teeth, and the appearance of being heavily sedated. People who are victims of sexual abuse can display behavior that is either overly sexual or extremely withdrawn.

Emotional and psychological abuse can be difficult to spot, but many victims of emotional abuse display signs of low self-esteem and a lack of self-confidence. They may also lash out at people around them. Children who suffer from emotional abuse often tend to get in trouble at school by acting out—some are caught lying, stealing, or fighting with classmates. In general, it helps for an individual to think about a specific set of questions: Do my family members care about me? Do I have enough food? Do I know where my family is when they leave the house? Am I treated with respect? If there is a tendency to respond negatively to such questions, there is a chance that person suffers from emotional abuse. If you know of anyone who needs help or advice, you can call Childhelp USA: 1-800-4-A-CHILD (1-800-422-4453).

Abuse can take many forms. This elderly man suffers from neglect.

someone with whom they had a relationship. Nearly one third of all women who visit hospital emergency rooms are treated for injuries related to long-term abuse. And, more often than not, these incidents occur in the place where the victims are supposed to feel the most secure—their own homes.

Additionally, studies presented in the 1993 Public Health Reports indicated that elder abuse is a major component of domestic violence. More than one million senior citizens in America are subjected to abuse and/or neglect every year. Many of these elderly victims are in domestic situations in which they are completely dependent upon their abuser.

Both the emotional and economic effects from this violent epidemic are substantial. Medical expenses that stem from the results of domestic violence total at least $3 to $5 billion each year. Another $100 million in wages and sick time is lost by businesses.

Domestic Violence as a Way of Life

Physical punishment within the family has a long history. The old expression "Spare the rod and spoil the child," for example, is meant as justification for using physical force in punishing a child.

Both wives and children have historically been considered the property of the family patriarch (male head of the household). In some countries, children and wives had no legal status and no way to protect themselves from abuse. Throughout history, mistreatment has been common. In eighteenth-century France, for instance, husbands were allowed to kick and beat their wives, as long as no permanent scars remained. A common saying during the era of Emperor Napoleon Bonaparte was "Women, like walnut trees, should be beaten every day." (Walnut trees were beaten or shaken so that the nuts would fall to the ground.)

In colonial America, British common law governed the abuse of women, especially the abuse of wives. In 1874, the supreme court of North Carolina ruled that when a husband "chastises" (punishes) his wife, "if no permanent injury has been inflicted... it is better to draw the curtain, shut out the public gaze, and leave the parties to forgive and forget."

However, in that same year, changes were made regarding children and domestic abuse. In 1874, the Society for the Prevention of Cruelty to Children (SPCC) was formed in New York City after church workers discovered a girl who was being abused by her foster parents. With no appropriate organization to turn to, the church workers contacted the Society for the Prevention of Cruelty to Animals (SPCA) and argued that the girl was part of the animal kingdom and therefore she deserved protection. It was not until the latter part of the 1960s, however, that all states passed laws requiring that cases of child abuse be reported to the police. In 1974, one hundred years after the creation of the SPCC, Congress enacted the Child Abuse Prevention and Treatment Act, which, among other things, established the National Center on Child Abuse and Neglect.

Some changes regarding abuse of women in the home began to occur in the United States in the late 1800s. The states of Alabama and Massachusetts outlawed wife-beating in 1871; by 1910, thirty-seven of forty-eight states permitted wives to divorce their husbands on the grounds of extreme cruelty. And in 1980, the Office of Domestic Violence was created by the Department of Health and Human Services.

Even with these many changes, in 1994 the Justice Department showed that in a high percentage of single-offender attacks against women, the attacker is a relative or partner. Also troubling, says John Stein of the National Organization for Victim Assistance (NOVA), is that the amount of violence has stayed the same since 1973, even

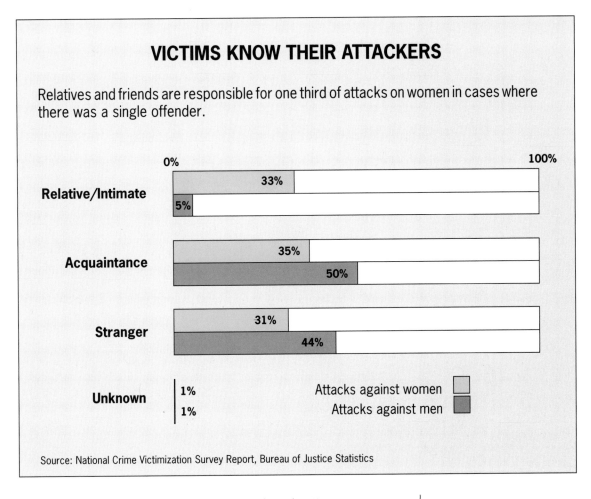

VICTIMS KNOW THEIR ATTACKERS

Relatives and friends are responsible for one third of attacks on women in cases where there was a single offender.

0%	100%
Relative/Intimate	33% / 5%
Acquaintance	35% / 50%
Stranger	31% / 44%
Unknown	1% / 1%

Attacks against women
Attacks against men

Source: National Crime Victimization Survey Report, Bureau of Justice Statistics

though stricter laws have been passed and a "vast network" of family violence services have been created across the country. And, although progress has been made, family violence remains a common problem in American society today. There is less social, and legal, control over the family unit than there is over individuals. Family matters are usually considered private. So lawmakers and police officers hesitate to get involved. And when they do step in, there is no guarantee that they will be able to eliminate the problem. A great difficulty in dealing with family violence is that it is experienced by people who claim to love each other. Victims thus often love, and want to protect, their abusers.

Chapter 2

The Batterer

Domestic violence knows no social, economic, racial, or religious boundaries. O. J. Simpson had wealth and fame. He had a beautiful wife and two children. He was, by most accounts, a man who should have been happy and fulfilled, but he wasn't. He was a batterer.

Axl Rose, the thirty-two-year-old lead singer and songwriter for the rock group Guns N' Roses, has also been accused of being a batterer. Rose has twice been the focus of domestic violence cases. Rose's ex-wife, twenty-eight-year-old Erin Everly, claims that throughout her four-year relationship with Rose she endured numerous beatings that left her bloodied and bruised.

Even the president of the United States has been touched by domestic violence. Bill Clinton's stepfather, Roger Clinton, Sr., was an alcoholic who physically and emotionally abused his family. In her autobiography, published after her death in January 1994, the president's mother, Virginia Kelley, described numerous incidents of abuse, including one in which her husband pinned her down and held a pair of scissors to her throat.

There is, then, no "typical" profile of a batterer. Abusers are found in every walk of life, and in every region of the country. They do, however, share many common

Identifying batterers is difficult because their behavior outside the home is often peaceful.

Opposite:
Most batterers have a tendency to abuse any member of the family who crosses his or her path. More than half of the people who abuse their spouses are also violent with their children.

characteristics. According to a 1993 report by the Family Violence Project in Reno, Nevada, eight out of ten batterers engage in violence against multiple targets—spouses, children, and parents are all in danger. In fact, more than 50 percent of all spouse abusers also abuse their children. Batterers often live in a state of denial: They do not recognize that they have a problem and usually deny the existence of violence in their homes. They often refuse to accept responsibility for their actions, instead choosing to blame some outside influence, such as job stress or abuse of drugs or alcohol. In fact, the annual football Superbowl has been shown to coincide with a major peak period of violence against women in the home. Some attribute this to excessive drinking that can accompany watching the game, or increased levels of aggression stimulated by the sport. Batterers also tend to be possessive and jealous, which leads them to isolate their victims from friends and family. Interestingly, most batterers also see themselves as victims. They often believe that they are the ones being overpowered, and that through their violent actions they are gaining a measure of control.

To the outside world, batterers often project an image of control and calm. They may appear to be completely normal. They do not necessarily lose their tempers at work or shout at strangers on the street—quite the opposite, in fact. Usually they function well in the real world; they do not appear to be "crazy." That is often because their rage simmers beneath the surface, boiling over only when they reach the privacy of their home and can exert control over vulnerable family members.

What are some of the reasons for abusive or violent behavior? Batterers typically become violent toward loved ones as a way to deal with their anger and frustration, or to improve their self-esteem. More than anything else, though, abusive behavior reflects a need for the batterer to regain control in a world where he or she may feel dominated and powerless.

"Battering is about maintaining power and dominance in a relationship," Dick Bathrick, an instructor at Men Stopping Violence, an Atlanta-based intervention group, told *Time* magazine. "Men who batter believe that they have the right to do whatever it takes to regain control."

To that end, batterers will not only physically assault their partners, but may also prevent them from leaving the house, visiting their friends or relatives, or talking on the phone. Sometimes the control is financial. Even though both people may be contributing equally to the family finances, the abusive partner will dictate how every penny is spent. Eventually, the person being abused begins to feel trapped, like a prisoner in his or her own home.

Artist Robert Markey stands with his scoreboard showing the football game score and the number of women battered during the Superbowl in 1993.

How Does a Person Become an Abuser?

Children who grow up in an atmosphere of violence come to accept the notion that abusive behavior is acceptable behavior. Day after day, they see evidence that "might makes right," and that the weak are always overpowered by the strong. This does not mean that people who are battered as children will automatically grow up to be batterers themselves. It does mean, however, that because they have become accustomed to witnessing or experiencing violence, and have been taught that abusive behavior is a normal part of a relationship, they are at greater risk to mimic that behavior once they become adults. In a 1993 Public Health Reports study of men who had been abused as children, half had grown up to be either convicted of a serious crime, mentally ill, or alcoholic.

One violence-control program in Minneapolis, Minnesota, reported an alarming statistic—80 percent of the male participants grew up in homes where they were either the victims of abuse or witnessed abuse. For years, psychologists and sociologists have speculated that children are traumatized by exposure to violent street crime. A report in the *Journal of the American Medical Association*, however, suggests that witnessing domestic violence has even greater consequences. "Boys become more abusive as adults; girls become victims," the report says. "Children of both sexes may come to see violence as an integral part of a close relationship."

In fact, there is some evidence that children who witness abuse in their homes may suffer greater long-term psychological damage than children who are themselves abused. In an August 1994 *USA Today* article, it was reported that children who are being abused learn to cope, day to day; those who see violence directed at a parent, however, can actually find it even more difficult to deal with. They come to see the world as a brutal and terrible place, where no one is safe.

Opposite:
Victims of domestic violence are often so controlled by their violent partners that they are cut off from everyone they know and love.

Some research even suggests a link between domestic violence and neurological problems. A study conducted by the University of Massachusetts Medical Center's domestic violence research center, for example, found that 61 percent of men involved in domestic violence showed signs of previous severe head injuries. It is possible that the damage left these men with a reduced ability to control their aggressive tendencies.

Another factor that can greatly contribute to the problem of domestic violence is alcohol and drug abuse. While the use of alcohol and drugs is not the *cause* of abusive

The use of drugs or alcohol contributes to the problem of family violence because it makes an abusive person more likely to lose control.

behavior, there is a consistent relationship between usage and heightened violent activity. People sometimes use alcohol and drugs as a way to forget their problems or frustrations. Unfortunately, the problems never go away. But while under the influence of drugs or alcohol, people may be more likely to lose control of their emotions and lash out in a violent manner. In a study prepared by the U.S. Department of Health and Human Services in 1994, the link between substance abuse and child abuse is very strong. It is estimated that nearly 10 million children under the age of 18 are abused by a parent who is under the influence of drugs or alcohol.

Economic stress, like alcohol and drug abuse, is also not a direct cause of domestic violence, but it often plays a role in aggravating cases of abuse. Losing a job or having trouble at work may cause someone to feel an overwhelming sense of pressure and frustration. Feeling powerless and vulnerable can cause someone to try to regain some sense of control over his or her situation, and can trigger abusive behavior.

A Violent Cycle

Abuse that takes place in the home is rarely constant. Rather, there is a cycle of violence that often occurs in three stages.

The first stage is something called the "tension-building phase," during which the batterer may use verbal threats, insults, and other forms of emotional abuse. Consciously or subconsciously, the batterer is trying to provoke a confrontation with his or her victims. The victims try to calm the batterer during this phase, in the hope of avoiding a major incident.

Eventually, though, the cycle progresses to its next stage, known as the "acute phase," during which the abusive behavior becomes extremely violent in nature. Uncontrolled rage is the most common characteristic of

Most batterers look for forgiveness from their victims—often by showering them with presents and apologies.

this stage. The batterer dominates, humiliates, and takes out every ounce of his or her frustration and anger on the victims.

Finally, there is the third stage, often referred to as the "honeymoon stage." It is during this stage that the batterer typically experiences overwhelming feelings of remorse, regret, and sadness. Some simply walk out the door after battering their partners. They try to "cool off" by going away for days on end. Others beg for forgiveness. They become very attentive and gentle, and shower their victims with love and affection. Often, they buy flowers and gifts. They may also take greater responsibility for household chores. In addition, they may treat their children with kindness and patience.

This stage is, in many respects, an attempt by the batterer and the victim to recapture the mood of the relationship when it was new, loving, and untarnished by domestic abuse. That is why it is often referred to as a "honeymoon" phase.

Some experts, though, believe "honeymoon" is too strong a word. They prefer to call the third stage the "hope stage." It is in this stage that both parties truly believe there is a chance to end the pattern of violence and save their relationship. They often hope that the most recent abusive episode will also be the *last* abusive episode. Unfortunately, in most cases, the cycle still continues. Eventually, the "honeymoon" ends and the tension begins to build again. Finally, the violent behavior is repeated. Each time the cycle is completed, there is less likelihood that it will ever be broken.

The batterer may still feel periodic shame and guilt, and probably will follow each violent episode with apologies and displays of affection. But the abuse becomes justified in the batterer's mind. It is learned behavior. And it is behavior that, to the batterer, is appropriate. Unfortunately, without counseling and treatment, this behavior rarely changes.

Chapter 3

The Victim

In the early 1980s, Charlotte Fedders was married to John Fedders, enforcement director of the Securities and Exchange Commission in the administration of President Ronald Reagan. After listening to Reagan discuss family violence in his 1984 State of the Union Speech, Fedders thought that the president might be able to help her.

Charlotte Fedders, as she explains in her book, *Shattered Dreams*, was a battered wife. She represents another example of the fact that domestic violence knows no boundaries. Her husband was a powerful and successful man, not the sort of man one would ever suspect of being a batterer. Fedders wrote a letter to the president in 1984. A year later she described her torment in a Maryland court, during her divorce proceedings. She talked about the multiple beatings that her husband had administered, and how, when they were still newlyweds, he had hit her so hard that her eardrum was punctured. She said that she tried to tell people what was going on, but no one, including her parents, wanted to listen.

On February 27, 1985, shortly after her court appearance, Fedders's story was reported in *The Wall Street Journal*. That same day, her husband resigned from his

Victims of domestic violence are found in all walks of life.

Opposite:
Charlotte Fedders, the wife of a successful politician, published *Shattered Dreams* in 1988 and shared her story of being a battered wife.

job. Although he publicly admitted beating his wife, Fedders was never charged with any crime. Charlotte Fedders obtained a divorce. Today, she works in a flower shop and lives with her four children. She is an example of the indiscriminate horror of domestic violence and, fortunately, she is a survivor.

As with the batterer, there is no typical profile of the victim of abuse. Battered victims come from all sectors of society—from every social, economic, religious, age, and racial group. There are, however, characteristics that are shared by victims. Frequently, abuse victims attempt to hide the signs of abuse from outsiders. Women may wear makeup and sunglasses to hide bruises, or long-sleeved shirts to cover scars.

Many victims of abuse often pretend that nothing is wrong. Even when directly asked if they are being beaten, they may lie. Some victims have been led to believe that somehow the abuse is their fault, and by acknowledging the violence, they would be admitting guilt of some sort. Others are simply too afraid to report the abuse, fearful that the abuser will only become more enraged and hurt them again.

A woman who is battered may also have been taught that it is a woman's obligation to keep a family together at all costs. She may come to believe that a broken marriage would represent failure on her part, and so she will stay in the relationship, even if it causes her extreme physical and emotional pain.

Victims of elder abuse also share common characteristics. For one, the recognition of their problem by society is relatively new. The term "elder abuse" was not even coined until the early 1980s. Elderly victims of domestic violence tend to be very frail, and nearly all live with their assailant, as opposed to being assaulted by a visiting family member. (Ironically, elderly victims often depend on their abusers for food and shelter.) Also, much of what is deemed elderly abuse falls into the category of neglect.

How Do People Become Victims?

We know that abusive behavior is learned behavior. What this really means is that people are not born either violent or mean; instead, they are taught these traits by someone whom they have had to watch being violent.

In much the same way that abusive behavior is learned, so is the behavior of the victim. People who have witnessed or experienced domestic violence as children are much more likely to become involved in an abusive relationship later in life. The reason is simple: They have become accustomed to coping with such behavior. A child who repeatedly sees her father abusing her mother may learn to believe that domestic violence is normal. This child may also then develop a distorted picture of human relationships in general, and of the role of women in particular, and can easily end up perpetuating the cycle of abuse from one generation to the next. Children who are abused, or who witness domestic violence, also often have impaired social and emotional development. They may have difficulty interacting with others.

The belief that abusive behavior is acceptable is one major reason why people tend to remain in violent relationships. Economic pressure is another reason. In many cases, the victim (especially a female victim) is completely dependent upon the spouse for financial support. If a battered woman is young and has children, she may be unemployed. Her partner is then responsible for paying the rent, buying groceries, diapers, baby food, and any other necessities. She may have few job skills and believe that if she leaves, she will be unable to find work. Without financial support, she may fear that she will lose her home and her ability to properly care for her children. This is especially true of women who have few people to turn to in a time of crisis.

Although help is available to abuse victims through government and private programs that provide counseling

Children who are abused often develop severe emotional problems and can become withdrawn, fearful, and even violent themselves.

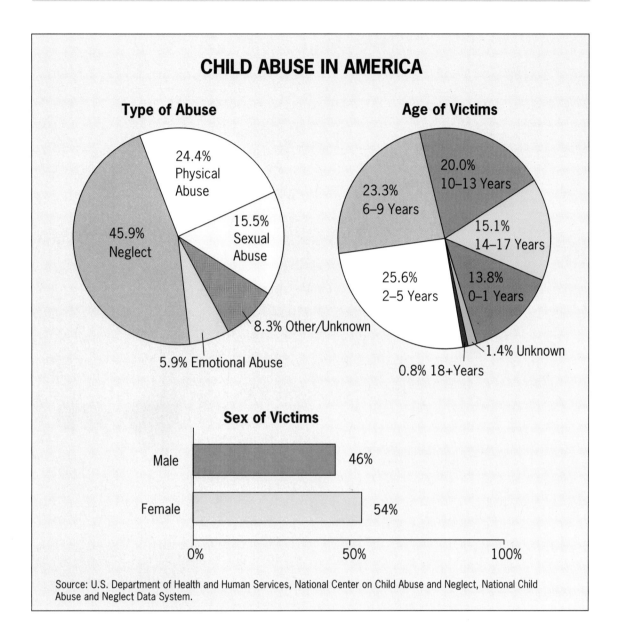

CHILD ABUSE IN AMERICA

Type of Abuse

- 24.4% Physical Abuse
- 15.5% Sexual Abuse
- 45.9% Neglect
- 8.3% Other/Unknown
- 5.9% Emotional Abuse

Age of Victims

- 20.0% 10–13 Years
- 23.3% 6–9 Years
- 15.1% 14–17 Years
- 25.6% 2–5 Years
- 13.8% 0–1 Years
- 1.4% Unknown
- 0.8% 18+Years

Sex of Victims

- Male 46%
- Female 54%

0%   50%   100%

Source: U.S. Department of Health and Human Services, National Center on Child Abuse and Neglect, National Child Abuse and Neglect Data System.

and protection, many may be unable to recognize exactly what their options are. Both fear and low self-esteem, caused by a long-term abusive relationship, can literally keep the victim from feeling that he or she is able to take action. The terror experienced by victims of domestic violence is quite real. Many carry with them each day

Husband Abuse

Because men are often bigger and stronger than women, they are rarely thought of as being victims of domestic violence. And, because a man who has been battered is far less likely to report the incident due to embarrassment, statistics on the subject are both rare and unreliable.

According to the National Council on Child Abuse and Family Violence, between 3 and 4 million women annually are the victims of violent assaults by husbands, ex-husbands, or boyfriends. In contrast, according to the Federal Bureau of Justice Statistics, the number of men who are assaulted by wives, ex-wives, and girlfriends is approximately 18,500. If accurate, that statistic means women are more than 200 times more likely to be abused by their partners. The figures, however, tell only a small part of the story, since they reflect only reported cases of assault. A few studies, including one published in 1986 by the *Journal of Marriage and Family*, indicate that not only do men and women assault each other in roughly equal numbers, they also murder each other in equal numbers.

Many experts in the field, particularly employees and volunteers at domestic violence shelters, will dispute that claim, arguing that when a women uses violence against a man, it is almost always in self-defense. Still, there is no denying that men are sometimes the victims of domestic violence. In 1975, the First National Family Violence Survey revealed that 4.6 percent of all husbands are struck by their wives.

When a man is the victim of abuse, he often suffers in silence. Many of these male victims of abuse feel that people will have very little sympathy for a man who allows himself to be physically dominated by his wife or partner. Abused men may feel that they are expected to either take control of the situation or endure the pain and suffering quietly.

the scars of emotional and physical abuse. They often survive from one day to the next, walking on eggshells, worrying that they will say or do the wrong thing and thus spark another attack.

According to the National Council on Child Abuse and Family Violence, battered women and children face the most physical danger when attempting to leave a domestic situation. They may even receive death threats. These threats are not to be taken lightly. Experts in the field of domestic violence note that the two actions most likely to prompt deadly assault on the part of an abuser are leaving a shared residence and starting a relationship with another person. Because of the serious risk involved, victims will often decide to remain in an abusive relationship, choosing to suffer in silence, instead of jeopardizing their lives to a greater extent.

Justifying Abuse

It is not unusual for victims of abuse to believe that they deserve the violence that is heaped upon them. Some victims, for example, routinely paint themselves as active participants in the abusive relationship, sometimes even suggesting that they provoked an attack. This is not true, of course. No one deserves to be beaten, killed, or abused in any way. And no one has the right to physically assault another human being.

Domestic Abuse—
The Impact on Children

Each year, about 3.3 million children are witnesses to violence between their parents. Studies have shown that both witnessing and experiencing domestic violence has traumatic effects on the lives of children.

• Children experience anxiety, fear, sleep disruption, and other kinds of emotional and physical disorders due to violence in the home.

• Abused children consistently have severe social problems that include having temper tantrums, trouble making friends, failing grades in school, and disciplinary problems both at school and at home.

• Children as young as one year may regress into states diagnosed as "mentally retarded" when exposed to severe verbal abuse in the home.

• Many children suffer low self-esteem, sadness, depression, stress disorders, poor impulse control, and feelings of powerlessness. They are also at high risk for alcohol and drug use, sexual acting out, running away, and suicide.

Many patterns of violence are learned early in life. Victims of domestic abuse may have a tendency to become either batterers or victims.

• Violent parental conflict has been found in 20 to 40 percent of the families of chronically violent adolescents.

• Adolescent boys exposed to domestic violence tend to use aggression as a means of problem solving. Girls, on the other hand, are more likely to display withdrawn, passive, and dependent behavior.

• For boys between 11 and 16 years of age, witnessing violence between their parents had a significant effect on delinquency, personality disorders, immaturity, and inappropriate behavior when attempting to solve personal problems with others.

Information compiled from studies presented to the National Resource Center on Domestic Violence.

Violence is not a proper or healthy reaction to either anger or frustration. Some studies, however, have found ongoing cases of domestic violence in which the victim seems to help perpetuate the vicious cycle. For example, a spouse may deliberately try to provoke jealousy and anger as an act of revenge. The batterer may then respond with violence.

Victims may contribute to the cycle in other ways. By continually forgiving the batterer and entering the "honeymoon stage," the victim does not help put an end to the violence. Later, when the abuse resumes, the victim may feel responsible.

People also tend to make excuses for the violent behavior of their family members. They do this for several reasons, not the least of which is the fact that they still love the person who is battering them. In some instances,

People involved in abusive relationships often experience cycles of violence. Unfortunately, forgiveness tends to keep the cycles going.

Abuse in Teen Dating

Studies indicate that abusive behavior among teenagers involved in dating relationships is becoming increasingly common. By the time they graduate from high school, one out of eight students will be battered by a partner; by the time they graduate from college, one out of five students will be battered. In a study published in the journal *Social Work*, one in four high school students were either abuse victims or perpetrators of violence.

While the behavior among young people in many ways mirrors that of domestic violence among adults, abuse in teenage dating is a uniquely disturbing problem. Peer pressure is a tremendous influence on most adolescents. Having a boyfriend or girlfriend may become one of the most important things in their lives. And when they are involved in romantic relationships, they may feel that jealousy or extreme possessiveness is not necessarily a bad thing. Jealousy may be misinterpreted by a teenager as a sign of love. A girl may believe that her boyfriend simply has a quick temper or that his angry outbursts are an indication that he truly cares for her, when in fact his behavior is inappropriate, dangerous, and abusive.

Even though they may have been exposed to similar behavior as children, adolescents do not consider domestic violence to be relevant in their lives. It is, to them, an "adult" problem. But an adolescent relationship can become just as abusive and harmful as an adult relationship. Adults often don't get the chance to help because victims may refuse to tell anyone what is happening, especially their parents.

"Teenagers tend to keep things like this from their parents. Their main relationship is with their own peers, not with adults," said a New York shelter counselor. "They feel mistrustful of adults, particularly their parents, because it's a time when they want to be independent. So talking about relationships with boyfriends and girlfriends, especially with parents, is something kids have a difficult time with."

Children from abusive households learn patterns of violence at an early age. They often begin to repeat these patterns when they start dating.

for example, a child may feel confusing emotions of anger and love toward an abuser, and those feelings of love may cause a child to want to protect an abusive parent. It is often difficult for people who have never experienced domestic abuse to understand how love and violence can exist within a single relationship, but that is often the case.

In other instances, though, failure to either press or drop charges may have less to do with love than fear. Victims of domestic abuse often have little faith in the criminal justice system. They do not believe the police will protect them because they are accustomed to hearing their cries for help go unanswered. They also believe the abuse will become much more intense when the batterer is released from jail—if, in fact, he or she does spend any time in jail at all.

It's Hard to Get Help

The sad truth about violence in the United States is that many people who are murdered are killed by someone they know—16 percent of the time by a family member, according to statistics in the 1993 Public Health Reports. In fact, 50 percent of American women who are murdered are killed by a current or former partner. And, in 1992, 1,100 children died from abuse or neglect. The home is not necessarily a safer place than the streets.

Sadly, family violence—child, spouse, elder, or sibling abuse—is not always treated as violence at all, but rather as a private matter between people who share a residence. Nothing more. A prevailing attitude is, "It's nobody else's business." As a result, this behavior that would be considered inappropriate or even criminal if it occurred in the workplace or on the street is not treated the same way when it occurs in the home.

For example, if a man loses his temper while at work, he generally knows better than to punch his boss in the face. The consequences for such behavior would be swift and severe. At home, though, if he hits his children or his wife, there may be no consequences at all.

The home may provide shelter from the outside world, but it may also serve as a strong barrier to those who are supposed to provide assistance. Violence in the home is considered assault; every state in the country has laws against child abuse. And yet, police respond to calls related to family violence much more slowly than they respond to calls related to public disturbances. This is partially due to the fact that dealing with domestic violence is usually dangerous work.

Some counselors and sociologists suggest, however, that police officers simply find domestic violence work to be distasteful. They do not like the idea of entering someone's home to break up what may or may not be anything more than an argument.

DOMESTIC MURDER

More than 9,000 of the 22,540 people murdered in 1992 were killed by people they knew. More than 3,000 people were killed by loved ones. Wives who were killed by their husbands made up the largest group of victims.

Wives (killed by husbands)
913

Friends (killed by friends)
843

Girlfriends (killed by boyfriends)
519

Other family (killed by family)
393

Husbands (killed by wives)
383

Boyfriends (killed by girlfriends)
240

Source: Department of Justice

Despite recent changes in some police policies regarding family violence, some officers do not consider it to be "real violence." They hesitate to intervene in an argument between a husband and wife because they suspect the charges will eventually be dropped anyway. They are also often reluctant to accuse someone of child or elder abuse because these charges are very difficult to prove. Thus, evidence that under different circumstances might lead to an arrest, such as a black eye, or bloody nose, or a terrified child clinging to the leg of his mother, is more likely to be ignored in the case of domestic disputes.

Incidents in which complaints of domestic violence are either ignored or treated as unimportant are all too common. But when the legal system trivializes the horror of family violence, the result is that abusers are allowed, if not encouraged, to abuse.

Esta Soler of the Family Violence Prevention Fund, a national non-profit group, says the criminal justice system

Police officers have a difficult job in dealing with domestic situations. Police policies are continually changing regarding family violence.

U.S. Attorney General Janet Reno contributed to improving the various ways in which domestic violence situations are handled by the law.

has limitations when it comes to reducing violence against women. "We can't expect just one institution to solve the problem," Soler says. "We still have a cultural acceptance of this type of violence—that's what we need to change."

Attorney General Janet Reno, who began a highly regarded domestic violence program while she was chief of the state prosecutor's office in Miami, has said that the Justice Department is studying ways to help local officials enhance prosecutions of violent crimes against women. "Cutting domestic violence could have an indirect effect on all violent crime," Reno says. "The child who watches his father beat his mother comes to accept violence as a way of life. If we're going to do something about violence in America, we've got to start at home."

Chapter 4

Breaking Free

traditionally, victims of family violence have received little help from our judicial system and law enforcement agencies. Although there are laws designed to protect the rights of children, the elderly, and spouses, cases often go unreported. And even when police are called to the scene of a domestic dispute, officers may be reluctant to make an arrest.

The Legal System

Domestic assault is often put into a different category than other types of assault. Until quite recently, official policy throughout the United States called for mediation (intervention with the intent to promote resolution to the problem), not arrest, in cases of domestic violence. Officers answering domestic dispute calls were expected to talk with the parties involved. If a victim was bruised or bleeding, it didn't matter. Police officers were expected to encourage a polite discussion; they were not expected to take anyone away in handcuffs. Many victims became so frustrated by this treatment that they chose not to call the police at all.

> Progress is being made to help end the suffering of abuse victims.

Opposite:
Laws regarding violent incidents in the home are becoming much stricter. In many states, officers are able to arrest suspected batterers more easily than in the past.

When arrests were made, charges were often dropped, or judges handed down extremely light sentences. This is what happened with O. J. Simpson, who, for his crime in 1989, only had to pay a small fine, do community service, and get counseling over the phone.

It is for this reason that victims have occasionally taken the law into their own hands: They feel as though no one is willing to help them. Such was the case with Becca Jean Hughes, who, in 1985, was found guilty of first-degree murder and sentenced to fifty years in prison after killing her husband, Don. Hughes claimed that her husband had been abusing her for years, and that she was acting in self-defense. A jury did not believe her.

Victims of child abuse have also turned to murder as a means of self-defense. One of the more infamous cases involved sixteen-year-old Cheryl Pierson of Long Island,

Cheryl Pierson was devastated by her father's abuse and feared he would abuse her younger sister. In 1986, she decided that the only way to stop her father was to have him murdered.

New York, whose boyfriend paid another young man $400 to kill Pierson's father, James. Cheryl claimed that her father had sexually abused her for years, and she feared that James Pierson was about to begin molesting her eight-year-old sister.

Cheryl Pierson was found guilty, but was sentenced to only six months in jail. That sentence seemed to reflect a tendency for juries and judges to be more sympathetic to the victims of child abuse than to the victims of spouse abuse. In both the Hughes and Pierson cases, though, it is clear that the abuse victims' violence came from feelings of desperation and hopelessness.

There have been changes in recent years. Before the O. J. Simpson case put domestic violence in the spotlight again, there was a movement to increase public awareness and create stricter guidelines for the handling of domestic disputes. In 1977, Oregon passed the first mandatory arrest law for an abuser in a domestic violence incident. More recently, the state legislature of New York passed the Family Protection and Domestic Violence Intervention bill in 1994 that mandated (legally ordered) arrest for any person who commits a domestic assault. The bill also required that police officers arrest anyone suspected of assaulting a spouse. People who opposed the bill said that arrest was not always neccessary and it deprived officers from using their own judgement. Today, officers called to the scene of a domestic dispute are not expected to merely lead a polite discussion; if one of the parties is injured, the officers are expected to make an arrest.

That same year, California's legislature fought for a computerized list of restraining orders (a legal order against a person to prohibit or restrict access to another person). A law was also passed that required judges to receive training in domestic violence. There was also a move in that state to take guns away from anyone arrested for domestic violence. In Colorado, a new set of domestic violence laws orders police to take abusers into custody at the scene. Also, anyone who violates a restraining order will be automatically arrested.

Also, programs that were activated in two cities—San Diego, California, and Duluth, Minnesota—succeeded in dramatically reducing spouse abuse. In these two cities, police were required to arrest anyone suspected of spouse abuse. Those convicted then had to have up to one year of

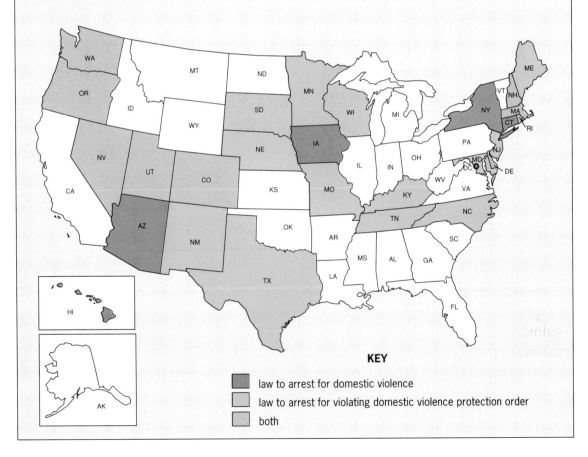

MANDATORY LAWS FOR DOMESTIC VIOLENCE OFFENDERS

The number of states that require police officers to arrest domestic violence offenders is continually increasing. In October 1994, at least twenty-eight states had a law for the mandatory arrest of a person suspected of attacking a family member or of someone in violation of a domestic violence protection order.

KEY

- law to arrest for domestic violence
- law to arrest for violating domestic violence protection order
- both

A Groundbreaking Decision

On June 10, 1983, Charles Thurman, Sr., drove to the home of Judy Bentley and Richard St. Hilliare in Torrington, Connecticut. Thurman's wife, Tracy, and their young son, Charles, Jr., were staying with Bentley and St. Hilliare. Tracy had moved out of the house after enduring many beatings at the hands of her husband. When Charles arrived he demanded to speak to Tracy; but she called the police, just as she had done many times before.

By the time a single police officer showed up, some twenty-five minutes after the call, Tracy had been stabbed thirteen times and was on the ground. The officer watched, stunned and frightened, as Thurman kicked his wife in the head and then ran inside to retrieve his son. He then dropped the boy on his mother's chest and bragged about having killed her. Three more police officers arrived on the scene, but allowed Thurman to wander free, ranting and raving, for several minutes before finally making an arrest.

Tracy Thurman survived the assault, though she remains scarred and partially paralyzed. She later filed a lawsuit against the city of Torrington and the police, arguing that they failed to provide her with equal protection under the law as guaranteed by the Fourteenth Amendment of the U.S. Constitution. It was Tracy's belief that police responded slowly to her numerous complaints against Charles because they did not really view domestic assault as a serious offense.

On June 25, 1985, a jury awarded Tracy $2.3 million in damages. Her son received $300,000. The case was appealed (brought to a higher court to be heard again) and Tracy later settled out of court for $1.9 million.

On June 10, 1986, exactly three years after Tracy was attacked by her husband, Connecticut Governor William A. O'Neill signed into law a family violence bill requiring police officers to arrest offenders in cases of domestic assault—even if the victim is unwilling to file a formal complaint. At the time, Connecticut was one of only eight states with such laws.

Charles Thurman, Sr., was arrested in 1983 for attempting to murder his wife. This case prompted Connecticut lawmakers to require mandatory arrests in domestic assault situations.

counseling. And if any counseling sessions were missed, that person then received a prison sentence. The results were promising—San Diego had a 60 percent decrease in domestic homicide and in Duluth, 80 percent of victims said that their spouses had stopped abusing them.

In Ohio, in 1990, Governor Richard Celeste ordered the release from prison of twenty-five battered women

Richard Celeste, former governor of Ohio, caused a stir in 1990 when he ordered the release of battered women serving jail sentences for attempted murder or murder.

What Happens to Reported Batterers?

Domestic violence offenders often do not receive consistent treatment by the legal system. Each state handles family violence cases differently.

• Maryland's Special Committee on Gender Bias in the Courts learned that many victims believe crimes involving domestic violence are not treated the same way as crimes in which the people involved do not know each other. The committee surveyed judges and lawyers in 1989 and found that 10 percent of judges said that the statement is always true and 14 percent said that it is often true. Also, 51 percent of male attorneys and 68 percent of female attorneys who deal heavily with domestic violence cases thought that the statement is either always or often true.

• Emerge—a Boston center that counsels men who batter women—estimated in 1992 that 65 percent of the men who join its groups are ordered to do so by a judge. In comparison, the center estimated that figure was only 5 percent in 1986.

• Of 781 domestic violence cases heard in Philadelphia Municipal Court between 1989 and 1990, only 67 cases, or 9 percent, resulted in conviction. Of the 67 people convicted, only 2 received prison terms.

• In contrast, in more than 3,800 family violence cases processed in 1990 in Connecticut, there were no findings of not guilty. The most common charges brought against offenders were breach of peace, assault, and disorderly conduct.

who had killed or attempted to kill their husbands. The reason for their release: They had been denied fair trials because expert testimony about battering and domestic violence was not allowed into evidence.

A sweeping and controversial crime bill, that went before Congress in the summer of 1994, also addressed the issue of family violence. Among other things, this bill sought to prohibit anyone convicted of a domestic assault from owning a handgun. This is especially noteworthy when one considers a startling 1993 study in the *New England Journal of Medicine*. This report stated that of all people killed by guns in their own homes, more than 75 percent were murdered by a relative or someone they knew. The amended crime bill that was signed into effect in September 1994, by President Bill Clinton, did include the provision that convicted batterers cannot legally own handguns.

Is There Hope?

We know that victims of abuse, even though they are suffering, generally find it very hard to walk away from the people who are battering them. People who have been subjected to years of domestic abuse often remain trapped in a situation out of fear for their lives. Victims of elder abuse and child abuse tend to believe they have no means of economic support, and so they choose to remain in abusive situations.

Sometimes, though, the abused break away from their abusers. Such was the case with Erin Everly, whose stormy marriage to rock star Axl Rose ended in the spring of 1990. According to Everly, Rose routinely punched and slapped her. On this night, though, after Rose allegedly beat her following an argument about their compact disc collection, Everly walked away.

"I didn't think I could survive mentally any longer," she told a reporter at *People* magazine. "I was dying inside. At the door I turned around and said, 'I want you to look at me, because you're never going to see me again.' And he never has."

Everly was fortunate. Her husband allowed her to walk out. Many victims of domestic violence discover that the battering escalates when they try to leave, and so they give up. For some, though, the pain of repeated batterings, and the constant feelings of fear, become too much to bear. They are willing to risk serious injury, even death, to get away from the person who is battering them.

This process takes time, of course. Many victims endure the cycle of abuse for years before even threatening to leave. They want to believe that things will change. When the situation worsens instead, they slowly come to the realization that the only way to end the violence is to walk away from it.

In some cases, a woman will leave a violent relationship only when she begins to fear for the safety of her children,

Opposite:
Rock star Axl Rose has a history of violence and has been accused of abuse by ex-wife Erin Everly. Here, Rose is arrested in July 1992, on charges of creating an outbreak of violence at one of his concerts.

Hillary Clinton and Janet Reno announced a study on the prevention of child abuse in August 1993.

as abusive spouses often abuse their children. Sometimes this fear is enough to prompt a battered wife and mother to break the cycle of abuse.

Children are in great need of relief from this problem. The Clinton administration has made the rights of children one of its platforms. In August 1993, Hillary Clinton and U.S. Attorney General Janet Reno announced a study called *America's Children at Risk, A National Agenda for Legal Action*. This report was created to give recommendations to the president, the executive branch, the judiciary, state and local governments, and attorneys on how to solve specific problems that relate to children. Five themes were discussed in this study, including the nation's need to devote more funding for preventive services for families in crisis. For example, families should receive counseling before children are taken away from abusive parents and put into foster homes. And family violence and substance abuse should both be formally recognized as public health problems in order to protect children from harm.

Coping

In October 1974, in St. Paul, Minnesota, three women opened the first battered women's shelter in the United States. It was called Women's Advocates. By 1985, there were more than 700 such shelters throughout the country. Today, there are more than 2,000 of them.

It is in these shelters that battered women find refuge for themselves and their children. In the dead of night, after an attack—or whenever the victim feels she is ready to ask for help—she can call a domestic violence hotline number. If she is unsure of the hotline number in her area, she can call 1-800-TRY-NOVA (1-800-879-6682), which

Hotlines are an effective way for victims of family violence to seek help. This Boston, Massachusetts, hotline operation, known as Samariteens, specializes in offering support to teenagers.

Working the Hotline

Hotline operators help people by giving them both emotional support and practical advice.

Roxanne Ramallo is the assistant director of Equinox Domestic Violence Services in Albany, New York. One of her duties is to answer the Equinox hotline, which receives some 250 calls each month. The hotline is in operation 24 hours a day, 7 days a week, 365 days a year.

According to Ramallo, there are often misconceptions about the type of person most likely to call a domestic violence hotline. "Most people think that when someone calls a hotline, they're crying, hysterical, they've just been beaten," she says. "That does happen, of course, but it's not usually the case. The majority of the calls we get are from women in hospitals, or women with police, or women who have made it out and decided to get help."

Some people who call a hotline are seeking immediate shelter. Before they are allowed access, however, Ramallo asks them a series of questions. First, she asks if they are in a safe place, where they can talk freely. Then she asks if they have a substance abuse problem, or a mental illness, or a serious physical problem requiring immediate medical care. The shelter, Ramallo explains, has limited space and resources, and some people would be better served by a hospital emergency room.

Not everyone who calls the hotline needs or wants shelter. "Some people just want to call and talk," Ramallo says. "Often it's the first time they're actually telling somebody what has happened. Once you make sure they're OK, then you listen to them. Just by listening you validate their experience. What you're telling them is, 'I believe you.'"

As the discussion draws to a close, Ramallo may raise the possibility of getting further help. It is not her job, however, to be judgmental or opinionated about the caller or the situation.

"We may, at the end, discuss some of her options," Ramallo says. "Maybe one of the options is, do you want to stay with a friend? Or, do you want to go to a relative? Do you want to come into the shelter?" But when a victim isn't ready to leave the battering situation, the counselor doesn't pressure her. "One of the things you have to remember when you're dealing with a battered person is that someone is taking power from them, and control," she says. "You have to give them the opportunity to come up with their own solutions."

is operated by the National Organization for Victim Assistance. Another national hotline, dedicated to domestic violence victims, was scheduled to be operating by 1995. That number would be available through the 800 operator. Battered children and men are also encouraged to use this hotline. Trained counselors talk with the victims, listen to their stories, and offer sympathy and support. For a victim who needs to get out of the house, but has no place to go, and no financial support, counselors can also direct that person to a shelter.

Shelters provide a supportive environment in which victims of abuse receive immediate protection, as well as food and clothing. Counseling services are also available at shelters. Here, victims have the opportunity, sometimes for the first time, to meet other people who have been abused. They discover that their stories are not unique.

Counseling is a crucial step in breaking the patterns of abuse. The Save Our Sisters shelter offers counseling to help victims overcome their many fears.

Children from abusive situations can also benefit from counseling. Here, a counselor engages a child in a practice called play therapy.

They support each other and share housecleaning and cooking duties. For a change, they live without fear: The location of all shelters is kept secret from the public, so that the abusers are not able to find and follow their victims. Life, though, is still not easy for most victims. Some abusers will try for many years to track down their partners.

Even when they manage to break free, victims of domestic violence carry physical and emotional scars for many years. Counseling can help them deal with the pain and to rebuild self-esteem. In the case of a woman with children, the financial and emotional stress of being a single parent can be overwhelming. Again, counseling can help, but it won't ease the burden of feeding and clothing a family and finding a suitable place to live.

Advocacy groups, such as the National Coalition Against Domestic Violence, which was formed in 1978, work to call attention to the problem of family violence. They advocate more federal funding for programs geared toward supporting the victims of abuse, and argue for tougher laws against crimes of domestic abuse.

Childhelp USA is one group that offers support to abuse victims—in this case, children. It is the largest, national, non-profit organization dedicated to the prevention, treatment, and research of child abuse and neglect. Sara O'Meara and Yvonne Fedderson opened Children's Village USA, the first residential treatment center just for victims of child abuse and neglect, in April 1978, in Beaumont, California. Today, Childhelp has offices in Los Angeles, California, Washington, D.C., and Knoxville,

Childhelp USA offers a safe haven for victims of abuse. Children benefit from a peaceful night's sleep at the Childhelp village in California.

Men are becoming active in a movement to help each other end their violent behavior. These demonstrators carried their well-intentioned, although misspelled, banner through the streets of Marin County, California.

Tennessee. In addition to operating the first Children's Village in Beaumont, this organization also runs the Childhelp National Child Abuse Hotline (1-800-4-A-CHILD) and adult survivor programs, as well as group homes for abused and neglected children in Orange County, California.

Help and counseling are also available for batterers. One such service is Emerge, a Boston-based program founded in 1979 for batterers. At Emerge, patients are urged to examine the reasons for their violent behavior, and to try to find other ways to deal with their anger and frustration. The program's success rate is approximately 20 percent, which might seem low, but is actually comparable to most drug and alcohol treatment programs. For those men who do seek treatment, and for their families, there is cause for hope.

Chronology

1871   Alabama and Massachusetts revoke the privilege of wife-beating.

1874   The Supreme Court of North Carolina rules that when a husband "chastises" his wife, "if no permanent injury has been inflicted... it is better to draw the curtain, shut out the public gaze, and leave the parties to forgive and forget."

1874   Church workers in New York City discover a girl who has been abused by her foster parents. The workers call the Society for the Prevention of Cruelty to Animals (SPCA) and argue that the girl is part of the animal kingdom and therefore deserving of protection and assistance. This leads to the formation of the Society for the Prevention of Cruelty to Children (SPCC).

1974   Congress enacts the Child Abuse Prevention and Treatment Act, which, among other things, establishes the National Center on Child Abuse and Neglect.

October 1974   In St. Paul, Minnesota, three women open the first battered women's shelter in the United States. It is called Women's Advocates.

1975   The First National Family Violence Survey reveals that one out of every six wives is struck by a husband at some point in their marriage. It also reveals that 4.6 percent of all husbands are struck by their wives.

1977   Oregon passes the first mandatory arrest law for an abuser in a domestic violence incident.

1978   More than 100 battered women's advocates from across the nation attend a U.S. Commission on Civil Rights hearing on battered

women in Washington,
D.C. They combine forces
and form the National
Coalition Against Domestic
Violence.

1980 The Office on Domestic
Violence is founded by the
U.S. Department of Health
and Human Services, in
response to the concerns
of millions of battered
women.

1990 Ohio Governor Richard
Celeste orders the release
from prison of twenty-five
battered women who had
killed or attempted to kill
their husbands on the
grounds that they had been
denied fair trials because

expert testimony about
battering and domestic
violence was not allowed
into evidence.

1993 A study published by the *New
England Journal of
Medicine* reports that of all
people killed by guns in
their own homes, more
than 75 percent were killed
by a relative or someone
they knew.

September 1994 A crime bill is passed that
addresses the issue of family
violence. Among other
things, it prohibits anyone
convicted of a domestic
assault from legally owning
a handgun.

For Further Reading

Cooney, Judith. *Coping with Child Abuse*. New York:
    Rosen Publishing Group, 1987.

Hyde, Margaret O. *Know About Abuse*. New York: Walker
    and Company, 1992.

Hyde, Margaret O., and Forsyth, Elizabeth. *The Violent
    Mind*. New York: Franklin Watts, 1991.

Kurland, Morton. *Coping with Family Violence*. New York:
    The Rosen Publishing Group, 1986.

Mufson, Susan, and Kranz, Rachel. *Straight Talk About
    Child Abuse*. New York: Facts On File, 1991.

Rench, Janice. *Family Violence: How to Recognize and
    Survive It*. Minneapolis: Lerner Publications, 1992.

Roy, Maria. *Children in the Crossfire*. Deerfield Beach, FL:
    Health Communications, Inc., 1988.

Index

Acknowledgments and photo credits

Cover: Leo de Wys; pp. 4, 44: Wide World Photos, Inc.; pp. 6, 58: ©Mark Richards/PhotoEdit; p. 8: ©E. Agostini/Liaison USA; p. 10: ©Pool/SABA; p. 12: ©Bill Aron/PhotoEdit; p. 13: ©Robert Brenner/PhotoEdit; pp. 14, 28, 48, 50, 53: AP/Wide World Photos; p. 18: ©Tony Freeman/PhotoEdit; p. 21: ©Bill Swersey/Gamma Liaison; pp. 22, 56: ©David Young-Wolff/PhotoEdit; p. 24: ©James L. Shaffer/PhotoEdit; p. 26: ©Mark Romine/Liaison International; p. 32: ©Sander/Liaison USA; p. 36: ©Amy C. Etra/PhotoEdit; p. 37: ©PBJ Pictures/Liaison International; p. 40: ©Laura Sikes/Stock South; pp. 41, 52: ©Dirck Halstead/Gamma Liaison; p. 42: ©Bill Bachman/Leo de Wys; p. 46: Map information from the National Center for Women and Family Law; p. 47: The Register Citizen; p. 54: ©Michael Newman/PhotoEdit; p. 55: ©Rhoda Sidney/ PhotoEdit; p. 57: ©Matthew Ford/Gamma Liaison.

Maps and charts by Madeline Parker/Blackbirch Graphics, Inc.